TRAINED TO **HATE** BUT DESIGNED TO **LOVE**

ACCURACY

Leviticus 19:18 Do not seek revenge or bear a grudge against one of your people, but love your neighbor as yourself. I am the LORD.

authorHOUSE®

AuthorHouse™
1663 Liberty Drive
Bloomington, IN 47403
www.authorhouse.com
Phone: 1 (800) 839-8640

Published by AuthorHouse 10/15/2015

ISBN: 978-1-5049-1794-0 (sc)
ISBN: 978-1-5049-1795-7 (hc)
ISBN: 978-1-5049-1796-4 (e)

Library of Congress Control Number: 2015909555

Print information available on the last page.

Contents

Do not seek revenge or bear a grudge against one of your people, but love your neighbor as yourself. I am the Lord.
—Leviticus 19:18

To my mother, the jewel of my life who is in heaven. It is you who I have always looked up to for my courage and strength. You instilled in me early on the Word of God. Had you not done that, I could have been reckless in my life. I haven't always gotten it right, but with you never far from my thoughts, I never wanted you to be disappointed in my actions or my disposition. I remember how proud you were of me when I came home and told you that I had joined the community church choir; the look on your face was priceless. With such a strong presence in my life, you gave me the courage of a bull and the presentation of a dove. I thank you for your guidance and your expectations of me. I look forward to seeing you in heaven. Love, your big baby, as you called me.

The Purpose of the Book

I will give firsthand accounts of incidents I experienced as a youth, adult, soldier, and law-enforcement officer, and I will give some examples of what I have experienced as a parent of African-descended male children, another story within itself.

The purpose of this book is to open your eyes to the seen and unseen racism that African-descended people experience on a daily basis. If you have any false pretense to the theme or facts of this book, look no further than our first African-descended president, Barack Obama.

On the day of his inauguration, as reported on the local news station, there was a group of prominent white politicians in a conference room across town making a pact to make President Barack Obama a one-term president. Why? Only one reason—because he is an African-descended person.

Why do they call him King Obama? I think it's because of their disdain for his origin and the fact that he is the president of the United States of America. Racist people deny America the opportunity to advance socially and economically, just to defy this president. Anyone who thinks like the group that assembled that night should hear this:

God Is the Ultimate Authority

"Let every soul be subject unto the high powers, for there is no power but of God: the powers that be are ordained of God" (Romans 13:1).

God Is Sovereign

"But God is the judge: he putteth down one, and setteth up another" (Psalm 75:7).

And at the end of the days I, Nebuchadnezzar, lifted up my eye unto heaven, and mine understanding returned unto me, and I blessed the most high, and I praised and honored him that liveth forever, whose dominion is an everlasting dominion, and his kingdom is from generation to generation. (Daniel 4:34)

This was said by Nebuchadnezzar, ruler of Babylon in the Chaldean Dynasty, who reigned from 605 BCE to 562 BCE. He conquered Judah and Jerusalem and sent the Israelites into exile.

God Instituted Human Government

"By me kings reign, and rulers decree justice, by me princes rule, and nobles, all the judges of the earth" (Proverbs 8:15–16).

Therefore, God will judge governments:

The kings of the earth set themselves, and the rulers take counsel together, against the Lord, and his anointed, saying, "Let us break their bonds and cast away their cords from us." He that sitteth in the heavens shall laugh; the Lord shall hold them in derision. Then shall he speak unto them in his wrath, and distress them in his displeasure. Yet have I set my kingdom upon the holy hill of Zion. (Psalm 2:2–6)

Therefore, to the government, I say, "Be wise, you kings; be instructed, you judges of earth. Serve the Lord with fear, and rejoice with trembling" (Psalm 2:10).

Immigration

Sojourn means to stay or visit, to live somewhere temporarily. Today, our political leaders appear to be struggling with the question of whom they will or will not allow to enter this country for the wrong reason. We need comprehensive reform in our immigration process. Our leaders need guidance in this matter. They need to be aware of their fundamental responsibilities when refusing a stranger entry into this country.

Leviticus 19:33–34 says, "When a stranger sojourns with you in your land, you shall not do him wrong. You shall treat the stranger who sojourns with you as the native among you, and

you shall love him as yourself, for you were strangers in the land of Egypt."

Now, you know the powers that are in this country have a real problem with opening up the border—and not just because of some of the ridiculous stuff you hear about immigrants. You hear people who oppose immigration, and let's say we are talking about the Hispanic population. Some of the people say the most hateful and racist things: "They come over carrying drugs, so that's why they have big calves." They also say, "They come over and rape our women and rob." One presidential candidate said, "Mexico is not sending us their good people." He went on to say that some of them might be good people. My heart wept for days seeing the way this country treated the young Mexican kids who had entered this country, fleeing one oppressive government only to run into the U.S. Government oppressive way. I say to you don't' think it couldn't happen to you next if they can deny one race then they will go for religion. Beware

Listen up—it's already been said.

Then I will draw near to you for judgment. I will be a swift witness against the sorcerers, against the adulterers, against those who swear falsely, against those who oppress the hired worker in his wages, the widow and the fatherless, against those who thrust aside the sojourner, and do not fear me, say the Lord of hosts. (Malachi 3:5)

I always try to keep in mind that if you are healthy and have received blessings, you should always be a willing servant for the less fortunate. You never know whom you may offend or help: "Do not neglect to show hospitality to strangers, for thereby some have entertained angels unawares" (Hebrews 13:2).

I'm glad we have people who give voice to the unfair way immigration is prioritized and how it's usually easier to enter the country if you are of European descent. They get support from the mainstream media. I heard a report on the local news about excitement about direct flights to Sweden, and it was deemed as a great thing. The same station demeans supporters of the Hispanic immigrant population, but I say to them: "Open your mouth for the mute, for the rights of all who are destitute. Open your mouth, judge righteously, defend the rights of the poor and needy" (Proverbs 31:8–9).

We have organizations out there fighting for the rights of the poor and having a leading voice in the championing of civil rights. One organization is the National Action Network, led by a man who is known for keeping it real. The good reverend pushes the easiest commandment of them all and the one that is greater than them all:

And you shall love the Lord your God with all your heart and with all your soul and with all your mind and with all your strength. The second is this: You should love your neighbor as yourself. There is no other commandant greater than this. (Mark 12:30–31)

Non-Native Americans may have a problem with opening the borders to other nationalities because of their own histories. We all know the stories of how America was taken from the Native American people. Today, the descendants of the first non-Americans to arrive in North America are still protecting that murderous heritage and have a fear that what their forefathers did to acquire the land will someday be reversed.

"And you shall make a response before the Lord your God: A wandering Aramean was my father. And he went into Egypt and sojourned there, few in number, and there became a nation, great, mighty, and populous" (Deuteronomy 26:5).

Last note on immigration: if politicians were serious about American citizens' protection from immigrants, especially the so called dangerous immigrants—or should I just say the people of color they should move forward with the immigration process trusting the Lord to guide them with un- bias eyes. You know, when the Republicans and their supporters talk about Hispanic immigrants, they talk about sending the entire family back across the border.

Doing the research for this book, I discovered that the US Government is paying deported Nazi war criminals Social Security. They are collecting US social security checks. Due to a so-called loophole, they have received millions of dollars in payments and still receive them today. The Nazi criminals made a deal with the U.S. Government. They agreed to leave the country if they could receive their social security—some loophole! The children of these criminals were not deported,

unlike the Hispanic kids who are being torn apart from their families. Again, look it up.

"He has told you, O man, what is good; and what does the Lord require of you but to do justice, and to love kindness, and to walk humbly with your God?" (Micah 6:8).

For those who will not allow immigrants to enter this country because of bias, hatred, and fear that they will be harmed by them: people are to seek the best for themselves and their families in this world, but be advised, they don't need your permission. The real citizenship is not of this world. "But our citizenship is in heaven, and from it we await a Savior, the Lord Jesus Christ" (Philippians 3:20).

Where is your true citizenship? If it's on earth then you will deny immigrants, but if you are seeking citizenship in heaven please consider what you have just read.

Function of Government

Judge with righteousness. "He will judge your people righteously, and the poor with justice" (Psalm 72:2).

The government will crush the oppressor, vindicate the afflicted, and support the needy. "He will judge the poor of the people. He will save the children of the needy and will break the oppressor in pieces" (Psalm 72:4).

The government should be responsible for the welfare of all citizens and show compassion. "He will have pity on the poor and needy: he will save the souls of the needy" (Psalm 72:13).

Are Your Politics Causing People to Be Poor?

Jeremiah 22:16 says, "'He judged the cause of the poor and needy. Then it was well. Wasn't this to know me, say Yahweh."

The word *cause* means a person or thing that acts, happens, or exists in such a way that some specific thing happens as a result—the producer of an effect. Are you causing people to be poor because of your political policies or your laws, or by disregarding the needs of poor people?

A Quiet Life with Tranquility

Allow all people to have a quiet life with tranquility. "For all kings and all who are in high places; that we may lead a tranquil and quiet life in all Godliness and reverence. For this is good and acceptable in the sight of God our savior" (1 Timothy 2:2–3)

Politicians that do harm for profit—and not good for the Prophet—will fall into despair.

These Republicans and their supporters hate President Obama so much they won't call him President Obama; they

say Mr. Obama. This demonstrates how ridiculous some of the chatter sounds.

If you were to ask any Republican or their supporters "Why do you oppose President Obama so much?" they would say anything to defame the president—something like "He's not American," or, "He thinks he's a king," or, "He wouldn't show us his birth certificate." They would probably say race has nothing to do with it in the end. *Wink*—okay, denial.

I always ask people what they mean when they say something with a racial undertone. Watch the response!

This is when you really get to explore the truth of a person's origin. Often, the answer will be baseless and flat-out idiotic. I will lay out my life experiences, and you will hear the echo of denial. A racist seem to get really dumb when they are confronted. They might even ask you, "Are you angry?" or, "Did I offend you." *No, idiot—you just gave me a compliment.*

Example: "Your teeth are so white, is it because of your dark skin?" it really happen.

Imagine that the so-called smartest race on earth can't recognize racism. When I say *they are the smartest race,* I am only speaking to the people who reserve these racist beliefs and violate human rights because of the race or religion of a person, or just pure hatred.

Quick question to the reader: do you watch *National Geographic* or any type of documentaries about animals? Give yourself a few minutes to ponder the question. Okay, by now you're probably wondering where this is going, back to the denial. Remember how I said they just can't seem to recognize their racism by denial.

I would like for you to plan to watch one of those extraordinary documentaries about animals. When you watch the documentary about animals. It doesn't matter what type of animal or species; just watch and listen to the narrator. Listen to how he explains everything the animals are doing. He will tell you what the animals are thinking, what they are planning, and even what the animals are feeling. Incredible—right?

No! Confusing. Why? They just can't seem to muster up enough patience, energy, or intelligence to understand another human being of a different race, particular African-descended people. *I'm shaking my head.*

Reaffirming the Purpose of the Book

Before I go any further, I would like to say the Lord's Prayer, I am praying that the words that I put in this book enlighten the reader of what a man of African descent endures in America every day—from causals to extreme incidents of racism—while trying to stay on God's path for salvation. I am praying that this book will be used to change the pattern of racism in America and the world. I want it to help people get past this dangerous disease before we all perish and never know how it could have been. If we just could have loved one another.

Can you please say it with me?

> The Lord's Prayer: Our father who art in heaven, hallowed be thy name, thy kingdom come, thy will be done in earth, as it is in heaven. Give us this day our daily bread and forgive us our debts as we forgive our debtors, and lead us not into temptation, but deliver us from evil: For thine is the kingdom and the power, and the glory forever. Amen. (Matthew 6:9–13)

Do you realize the Bible speaks of bias at least twenty times?

John 7:24 says, "Do not judge by appearance, but judge with right judgment." The following are verses that deal with bias:

Galatians 3:28, John 7:24, Romans 10:12, 1 John 2:9, James 2:9, Genesis 1:27, Romans 2:11, John 13:34, 1 Corinthians 12:12–13, Colossians 3:10–11, Acts 10:34–35, Matthew 7:12, Ephesians 6:9, Revelation 7:9, Luke 10:25–37, Luke 10:29–37, Ephesians 2:14–15, Song of Solomon 1:5–6, James 2:8, Numbers 12:1–10, 1 Samuel 16:7.

I have placed these verses because I want the reader to understand the origin of my passion. It is guided by the living word of God, which is fit for reproof.

Chapter 1

CHILDHOOD

I grew up in China, a very small town in Texas. It is the county seat, where you get licenses, vote, and pay taxes. China sits fifty-four miles north of Bile, Texas, and 150 miles northeast of Newsome, Texas. The town is home to approximately 1,200 residents. The breakdown of the population by race in 2000 was 802 whites (61 percent), 383 blacks (32.1 percent), five American Indian and Alaskan (0.4 percent).

When you look at the population and the breakdown by race, you can determine that this is typical of the population in rural towns of America. The terminology is changing from *rural* towns to *suburban* towns, but the concept is the same—fewer minorities, better schools, safer communities, and a sense of neighborhood.

China is a town built on a strategy of division, and it's not indicative of the strategies throughout this country. From the sixties until the early nineties, China's minority community lived in a part of town separated by railroad tracks from the white community, and between the three main streets. The community was and still is surrounded by the white community. The white community calls the community "the quarters" or "across the tracks." Down South, if you want to find an African-descended community, you can use those navigational terminology.

China was a fun place to grow up as a kid. There was a lot of freedom in this small town, in terms of being able to move around in the community without fear. In my community, everybody knew everyone, and we had a village mentality. The older kids would take care of the younger kids, and parents shared information about their kids, so you couldn't get away with anything. When you got caught doing wrong, you would get punished by whoever caught you and then by your parent—and it could be just for swearing.

We had an area where we played sports. There were a couple of goals and some beat-up swings with broken chains and hanging seats. We called it "up on the mountain." It was the minority community park. There wasn't much to it—no grass or lights. We would go up on the mountain after school and shoot basketball until dark, as there were no lights to continue the game or any other activity.

On the other side of town in the white community, they had a park with lights that included a swimming pool, a tennis court, and a basketball court. I'm not sure if we were banned from going to that park or not, but I think it was understood that it wasn't our park, and we didn't go there.

One day, my friend Tiger and I decided that we were going to that park to swim. I don't know what led us to do it, but we did; we went there, and I think we had to do some explaining. I'm not really sure of the dialogue, but we paid the people at the gate and entered. When we entered the building to shower, as directed by the doorkeeper, the people looked at us a little funny, like *what are you doing here.* We ignored them and proceeded to the shower, after showering, we entered the pool area and got into the pool. I noticed a few people getting out of the pool, but for the most part, there wasn't much commotion in response to our presence.

That day, Tiger and I were the first minorities to swim in the white community's swimming pool in China. I guess you can say we were trendsetters, or we broke the color barrier.

Today, I must report to you that China has changed in some areas; the tracks are gone, literally and figurative. They are no longer there, and the minorities have now moved to the other side of the tracks and to the other side of one of the main streets, into the white community.

Integration seemed to be catching on—better late than never. I visited China in October 2013 and found it to be evolving. The people seemed to be friendly and cordial toward one another. I even saw whites and blacks living in the same apartment complexes. Yet there were still strong boundaries when it came to race relations.

Neighborhood planning based on this model is the template for America's continued racist divisions, thus creating unequal communities while expecting the pride of all citizens to be the same.

There is a comprehensive plan in place to continue this pattern of racism in America—reverting monies from what would support these inner-city local schools and redirecting it to charter schools built on the ideology of separation, security, and the fear of the influence of African-descended children's "devilish" ways. Boo!

I'm amazed at how the residents of these suburban communities respond to crime in their neighborhood. They will come out and say, "I didn't think this would happen in this community, in such a good neighborhood where everybody gets along." It seems to imply this is a good place because we don't have all the minorities. This isn't just my thought; you can ask any African-descended associate if you know one or work with one or wherever your encounter may be. Just ask them honest and think it will make a difference they may tell you.

Let me remind you, my friend, you are policed differently, and therefore you are not included in the daily statistics or on the evening news with the caption "Crime News." Don't be fooled by the statistics of the law enforcement and the presentation of the media, even though the prisons are full of minorities.

Incarcerated Population

The largest population of inmates in this country is whites. If you are talking population percentages, you will see higher numbers of minorities due to the fewer amount in the population. According to the Federal Bureau of Prisons, as of June 27, 2015, whites accounted for 59 percent of the prison population (122,782 inmates), while African Americans made up 37.5 percent (78,021 inmates). Asians and Native Americans rounded out the incarcerated population at 1.5 percent (3,186 inmates) and 1.9 percent (3,973 inmates), respectively.

White Americans make up a large portion of the population, thus their percentage is lower from their population. So beware of false security; you are also being locked up at an alarming rate. You are more likely to be harmed by someone in your own race or in your own community than by someone of any other race. People usually get killed in their own environment or own neighborhood.

I experienced racism at an early age, growing up in Texas. There were many incidents, but I will talk about the ones that I keep in the back of my mind, the ones that had a strong influence on the way I view race today and how I respond to racism. The incidents that follow also demonstrate Reasons to be involved with your children's activities.

When I was about seven years old, I was playing Little League baseball. My team was getting ready to play the championship game, and I went to the concession stand to get some refreshments. I was stopped by one of the kids from the opposing team that we were supposed to play in the championship game.

This was a white kid, and he was talking trash while sitting on the back of his daddy's flatbed truck. The trash talking got to be a little personal. I could tell he was getting very angry, as his face and ears were getting red, and I was also getting angry. The kid called me a nigger, and I walked over to his dad's truck and pulled him off. He hit the ground. That was a big mistake.

When the kid hit the ground, he started to cry, and that was trouble because the kid's father got extremely angry and started to chase me. I ran. The man's face was very red, and he chewed tobacco and had creases in his face along his jaw. The cress in his jaws were so deep you could see the tobacco spit stain in the groves of his face.

This man chased me around the school with a knife in his hand, saying that he was going to cut my throat. I ran around the baseball field, across the baseball field, and through the parking lot. I was so terrified, and no one was trying to stop this crazy man from hurting me. I ran from him until the game started.

I continued watching him throughout the entire game and was still terrified. Not knowing this crazy man's limit or what he was capable of made it even more frightening.

The most revealing thing was I didn't get any help from anybody at the local high school, which was where we played our games. No help at all—not even from the coaches, fans, or parents, who were all white.

The lack of compassion and refusal to help a young African-descended kid was very telling. These thing have happened and will continue to happen with the same silence. A kid should be enough reason for someone to help. I had to make my way home after the game alone, still very afraid of this man. I ran all the way home, about a mile away.

I often think he could've done anything to me and would have gotten away with it. This book is being written after the *Trayvon Martin vs. George Zimmerman* case. A white adult male shot and murdered an unarmed sixteen-year-old black child and got away with it. Like President Obama said, "I could have been Trayvon Martin forty-one years ago." I have seen the man that chased me that day many times since that incident. I must say I don't have any hate in my heart toward him. I will leave it to God.

Romans 12:19 says, "Beloved, never avenge yourselves, but leave it to the wrath of God, for it is written, 'Vengeance is mine, I will repay, says the Lord.'"

Thanks to that incident, I can count on one hand the number of events I missed while raising my kids as they participated in youth sports. Hopefully that will inspire you to do the same. Kids are resilient in the way that they experience life. When they go through something, they may or may not speak of it, so for parents, it's very important that you go where your kids go. I did not tell my mom about this incident because I feared for her, and if you knew my mom, you would know she would have given that man the what for. Parents, be there to protect your kids. Black kids alone in today's America have about as much chance as a lamb in the South Africa jungle.

My truth, my proof—too blessed to be stressed.

Wrong neighborhood? Or as law enforcement characterizes it in their terminology and training, belonging.

This childhood experience came when I was in the fifth grade while living in Joe, Florida. It was during football season. I remember that because the incident happened when my brother Jim and I were walking home from a football game. Jim was in eighth grade at the time. We were walking home and were approached by two white males driving a large truck why. I could take a guess, but I will let your imagination fill in the blank. However, on one occasion we did play a predominant white team, and they were good. They beat us, and that was impressive, as we didn't lose many games.

On the Saturday night I began telling you about, we stopped at the local market. I think it was called Senior Food Store or something like that. We went in and made our purchases. A white guy we knew from school was in the store. I'll call him Mike, we played football with him.

Change is a continuous process. Mike departed the store before we departed and had driven off before we exited the store. We departed the store, and when we got outside, two white men greeted us. We knew both of them; they went to school with our older brothers. One of the men stood about [f]oot five with long hair and a beard, and the other stood [ab]out five feet—if that. He was very small. They claimed that [on]e of us had said something rude to the white girl who was [wo]rking at the store.

[Th]is is where it gets tough. I knew the short guy's brother, and [co]nsidered his brother a friend. We played football together [as k]ids, and he was a tough kid. I depended on him, and he [dep]ended on me on the football field. I thought it would have [put a] strain on our relationship if I told him what happened. [Plus], it wasn't him; it was his brother, and I didn't get the [feeli]ng that he was that type of person.

with large wheels. The men in the truck drove up near us, slamming their brakes, and the wheels on the truck made a high-pitched squeaking sound. They said, "Come here, niggers." They yelled racial comments at us, and my brother and I ran across the street into some woods. We were terrified.

I found a bottle in the woods, and I broke it to protect myself. When I broke the bottle, I cut my left hand. It started to bleed, which terrified my brother and me (I still have the scar on my left hand as a reminder of that terrifying night).

We stayed in the woods as these men drove up and down the street, yelling, "Come here, niggers!" It seemed like an eternity. Eventually they decided to leave, and we came out of the woods and ran for about two miles to a theater where one of my dad's friends work, a gentleman named Carl. We stayed with him until he finished working at the theater, and then he took us home.

I was still terrified by the incident when I got into bed that night. Once in bed, I heard the traffic of the neighborhood and some wheels making that high-pitched squeaky sound. I started sweating and returned to the fear of the earlier incident.

Think about it; it only happened because they saw two helpless black kids walking alone in the wrong neighborhood or out of bounds. They wanted to do what every racist dreams of, which is to harm a black person—preferably one who is helpless. That's what they look for; that's what cowards do.

Quick Story

I saw a picture of a Ku Klux Klan member covered in a white sheet. I thought it looked like a ghost. I thought, Man, this is scary. Then an old African-descended man told me that it was a man. I asked, "Why is he covered in a sheet?" The man said, "Because cowards like to hide behind their sheets and do bad things, and with the sheet, they hide who they really are."

Belonging

I hear people say how afraid they are to walk the streets in some communities. Specifically, I hear some white people say they are afraid to walk in African American communities. I will say to you that I will walk up and down any African American community and fear nothing, except the police possibly stopping me. Now I will not walk in a white community alone at night. It's just dangerous, and to be honest, it's suicide.

I am cautious about walking in white communities because the threat of something happening to me goes up 100 percent. I could be harassed like in the previous story. That evening, I was walking in a white community. The fact that I'm in a white community creates suspicion among the residents. My fear someone will call the police and report a suspicious person. "A black man is walking down the street and acting strange." That's all it would take. So basically I'm saying I can walk in African American communities with no fear, but when I'm in white communities, I walk with caution and fear.

How do you navigate this path in your life? Do you shar same experience in your journey of life? If you are hu I'm sure you have had similar experiences. Whether other people believe you, I do, and I hear you. Evil color barriers!

My truth, my proof—too blessed to be stressed.

The Noose and the Knife

I start this childhood incident with chills not be forthcoming incident was so terrifying—they all because I have an inventory of these racist incident from. Wow.

This childhood incident involved two of my friends, whom I'll call Dan and Slow to protect t

It was a late Saturday night in China, and the th returning from some youthful fun out of tow were about sixteen years old, and Slow had a ni 1974 Pontiac Grand Am, white with maroon l We were returning from New Orleans, whe finished watching a softball game in which c team was playing.

We always went and participated in the Com League, specifically softball. The league wa We didn't have any white members on our c and we usually didn't compete against th

So why would I place that racist incident on him? I wouldn't do that. It's not who I am or what I am about. You are not your brother, and he is not you. So you deserve your own evaluation based on your actions, not someone else's. Unfortunately, for African-descended people, there is a concept that if one is bad, they're all bad.

So they were claiming that one of us had said something rude to the white girl, and they were demanding that we go back in the store so they could investigate. While shouting out these commands, I noticed the tall guy had a rope in his hand, tied into what appeared to be a noose, the hanging kind, and the short guy had a knife in his hands.

The short guy stated, "You boys got to pay for that. Which one of you niggers was talking to the girl?" We were very concerned and aware of what was happening, so we didn't say much as we cautiously got into Slows car so we could get out of the area. We managed to get in the car, and we were blessed to get out of there unharmed and without having to defend ourselves physically.

These cowardly types of people will talk their way out of things if they see they're not getting the response they're looking for, which is fear. We showed no fear as we departed. We had the power of God with us!

Psalm 23:4 says, "Even though I walk through the valley of the shadow of death, I will fear no evil, for you are with me; your rod, and your staff, they comfort me."

That's why we were blessed. When you walk with the King, the King of Kings, you don't have to be afraid. The thing I took from this incident still holds truth today. The white woman has been an excuse for the rage among racist people.

In some cases, the racist will lie about the woman. Yes, the racist will lie on the woman to inflame fear and provoke violence in a community, and she will allow it. Why? Preservation or fear?

Remember the Black Wall Street (aka Greenwood) in Tulsa, Oklahoma, on May 31, 1921, an African-descended man was accused of an assault on a white woman, and the rest is buried in black history and never mentioned in American history. It is estimated that between 1,500 and 3,000 black people were killed—business owners, veterans, doctors. This was because of a lie about an African-descended man approaching a white woman. Then you see a young racist, twenty-one years old, enter a church in South Carolina and kill nine people, including a beloved politician. I don't understand why they haven't called his death to this day an assassination. The young man entered a historical house of worship that played a major role during America's enslavement of thousands of African-descended people. Statements made by this murdering racist include "you are taking our women" and "you are taking over our country." Please educate these young men in love. I believe when you see young men commit violate crimes like that they are trained to hate. Someone should tell them they are designed to love. It is the free will provided to us by God. Between 1,500 and 3000 African-descended Americans were killed with no explanation and no retribution, and no one was jailed.

Domestic Enemy

America swears to protect its citizens from enemies both foreign and domestic. This means they have to classify the KKK as a domestic terrorist group. They have killed more Americans than the Taliban and ISIS combined, with no retaliation from our federal government. Compare that to the Twin Towers in NYC.

Then we got these idiots talking about four Americans (white men) being killed in Benghazi, and they speak of impeaching President Obama. We should go retro and impeach every president in the history of this country if that's the standard for impeachment, because none of them have declared war on this domestic terrorist. The conflict is that they'd be declaring war on themselves, and you'll win the lottery before that happens.

My truth, my proof—too blessed to be stressed.

This next story is number four, but in no way is it the fourth incident of racism at this point. I point that out because this will cover my last childhood incident for the purpose of the book, and I say that to reaffirm that even at the tender age of sixteen, I had an inventory of racist incidents to choose from.

Institutional Racism

I'm going to use this next incident as my introduction to institutional racism, and you probably will not be surprised to know that my first experience was with the American public school system. Yes, the white kids get to do what they want, and kids of color get to follow the rules or get punished when they don't.

You can visualize this story. I was a member of our local high school football team, the Panthers. I thought I was pretty good, but that's always debatable. One thing I won't debate is my role as a leader on the team and as a leader for many other students.

I made it my business to communicate to everyone who would listen. I felt I had a gift to respond to and communicate with all people on all levels. I got a great feeling talking to some of the special needs students.

I remember how excited they would get just because I played on the football team, and I would spend time talking, laughing, and just socializing with them.

I remember one of the guys. His name was Ennos. He was full of energy, and every time I spoke with him, he got very excited. I think he inspired me as much as it appeared to make him happy when I used to talk with him.

When you talk about institutional racism, you can describe it as a system of inequality based on race and how it governs it members, on the basis of institutional norms. Remember that as I take you through my experience.

On game day, the Panthers had a tradition of keeping the team isolated from outside influences. In other words, you couldn't leave the school property until after the game that night. This was only for home games. When games were played out of town, we normally left before school was out or immediately after school.

With a home game, we would get a meal after school from the school's cafeteria, and after the meal, *all* students were to stay in the auditorium until it was time to go to the locker room and get dressed for pregame warm-up. On this day when we had a home game, I noticed a lot of traffic among the white players. They were going in and out of the auditorium, and I noticed they had been to the store.

I thought we were all cleared to go to the store because the white players didn't appear to be concealing their purchases. So I decided to walk to the store.

I walked to the store; we used to say, "I'm going uptown." So I went uptown, bought some candy and bubblegum, and headed back to the school. While I was walking back to the school, I saw one of the assistant coaches driving by in his truck. He didn't say anything, just gave me a stare like *what are you doing*. When I returned to the school, the head coach called me to the locker room and coach's office.

When I arrived in the office, all the coaches were there—four white coaches. They wanted to know who gave me authorization to go to the store. I explained to them that the white players were going to the store in theirs trucks, so I thought it was okay to go to the store. I didn't see anyone come into the auditorium and authorize them to go to the store, so I didn't think I needed permission.

It became apparent in the coach's next statement that we had a difference in our understanding of the rules of this institution and the applications of them. The coach's next words were "You will have to get a paddling" (get hit with a piece of wood on your butt). Believe it or not, that was a punishment in the eighties.

I respectfully (hopefully) told the coach I wasn't going to accept the punishment because he didn't punish the white players. He gave me a choice. He said I had to accept the punishment or I couldn't play football. Needless to say, I quit football that day—not because I wanted to but because I was forced to stand up against a racist practice that had probably gone on for many years prior to me standing my ground.

I didn't want to quit. I was forced to quit, and that burned my soul. I have never wanted someone else to control my destiny, and these four men managed to do that for one day. The fact that these four men forced me to choose to protect my civil right over a football game gave me a clear understanding of what my rights meant to them—absolutely nothing.

The game was played on a Friday, and I had the whole weekend to redirect my energy in a positive way. I was always good at recovering from setbacks, and this was just another one. That weekend, I kept going over the situation to determine if I should have done something different, and I kept coming up with the same conclusion—not to accept the punishment.

I also had the image of these four white men sitting there trying to encourage me to accept the punishment, and not one of them had the courage or cared to support or defend me. That made me angry at all of them, not that it would matter to them. That day, they all turned into kids; it was like bullies picking on a helpless kid. This was my first experience in a kangaroo court—a mock court where the principles of law and justice are disregarded or perverted.

I made it through the weekend and went back to school on Monday. The coaches were also teachers at the school, and I had classes with a couple of them. I went to their classes, conducted my business as a student, and didn't talk sports with them. In fact, I don't recall speaking to them. Over the weekend, I had decided to talk to the head coach, so I waited until after school. I didn't want to engage any of the other coaches until I was able to speak to him; I didn't want them to give him a heads-up.

I wanted to use the element of surprise to ask this question. I called it the million-dollar question. I didn't want to have small talk with them because I wanted them to see me as a person and take my question seriously, and I wanted to catch them off guard or ambush them as they had done to me on Friday. The last bell rang, and I went straight to the coach's office. I asked him if I could speak to him, and he allowed me to.

The first thing I did was apologize for going to the store. I went on to say, "I didn't think it was fair that you wanted to punish me for going to the store, and you did not punish the white boys." I then asked if I could return to the team and reemphasized that it was not right to punish me for something that wasn't equal.

I'm sure there was a pause, possibly a little shock, and he was definitely impressed. To my surprise, he allowed me to return to the team.

You know what's really funny about that? I spoke with one of those coaches in the summer of 2013. We talked about that incident, and he said he remembered it. I would be remiss if I didn't tell you that I consider that coach a dear friend today.

We often talk about going through things to either make us better or to prepare us for something greater, and I agree with that theory. I agree because, as a parent, I had similar situation with my kids. I saw them coming into contact with rouge coaches, and I was equipped to deal with the problems, and I eliminated them. You will hear those stories when I get into the parenting phase of this book.

My truth, my proof—too blessed to be stressed.

Chapter 2

ADULTHOOD

Becoming an adult in America for some African-descended people is a milestone alone. Young African-descended males are being gunned down by themselves, strangers, family members, and by the forces that are supposed to protect them—the law enforcement.

According to a study by the Bureau of Justice Statistics, between 1978 and 2011, there were 279,384 black murder victims, resulting in a 94 percent figure.

In a Mother Jones report, the NAACP reported that in forty-five officer-involved shootings in the city between 2004 and 2008, thirty-seven of those shot were black. None were white. One-third of the shooting resulted in fatalities although no weapons were found in 40 percent of the cases. The report also found that no officers were charged with any of the fatalities.

When I say becoming an adult in America as an African-descended male is a milestone, I'm not kidding. More importantly, who cares? I will direct you to the following: "The Lord will rescue me from every evil deed and bring me safely into his heavily kingdom. To him be the glory forever and ever Amen" (2 Timothy 4:18).

My adult experiences will simply cover nonprofessional incidents, meaning not at a workplace. The reason for the distinction is that my work history started immediately out of high school when I joined the Texas National Guard in 1984 at the age of eighteen.

Causal Racism

Some experiences of racism are what I call causal racism. For example, it's when you're waiting to get a parking spot, and a white lady comes from another direction of the parking lot and pulls in before you and calls you a "stupid nigger" because you were trying to tell her you were waiting for that spot.

Another example is when you're leaving the store and you pass an older white lady on your way out, and she clutches her purse and tightens the strap on her shoulder.

Uniform Identifier

I stated earlier that I had joined the Texas National Guard. I want to distinguish my encounters or experiences stated above with this distinction. In most of my daily movements in the public while in uniform, whether it was my military or correctional uniform, the responses were much different. I had little to no reactions as stated above, and they were definitely not racial.

Effects of Racism

This will give you an idea of the psychological effects of these racist practices. For the racist, he is always suspicious of the African-descended male unless he can easily identify something of content, like a job or activity. Unfortunately, just passing a person, you don't always get that type of information, unless through a uniform or some type of insignia or professional identifier.

For the African-descended male, he is constantly checking himself, surveying his surroundings and praying that he is not being misunderstood by what he's wearing or how he's moving. I must say that it is very exhausting and senseless. Animals have more comfort in their day-to-day passing than God's prized possession, humans.

Love Thy Neighbor

In 1996, I purchased a home in Ohio in a community that sat along an industrial area, very quiet. The thing I noticed when I moved into my home was the number of elderly people in the community. I would be remiss if I didn't mention that I was the second African-descended family to move into the community.

The neighbors that lived next to me—my only neighbors since my house was on the corner of the block—were the first to greet and speak. It wasn't an "Hello, welcome to the neighborhood." It was more like "Hi, my name is Melina, and this is Resard, and we were wondering if you wanted to go half on a fence." They wanted to construct a fence between the two houses.

That struck me in a strange way and made me wonder how long they had lived here. The other question was when they decided to put up a fence. I inferred that because I was of African descent and had young kids, they made it clear that they wanted a separation. I respectfully let them know that I wasn't interested in a fence.

In the months that followed, the neighbor constructed a fence; thus, separation was established. This guy saw the young African-descended kids and probably thought they were going to be all over his property, playing and destroying his property and burglarizing their home.

None of that happened, but it did give me an opportunity to teach my family about discrimination as it relates to housing (Title VIII of the Civil Rights Act of 1968).

Later on, I had an opportunity to meet other neighbors in the community. One was a white man in his seventies named Blay-fry. He was the type of guy who would say anything—just speak without thought or care. One day I was out on the front lawn with my boys and a couple of my nephews. The kids were around nine to eleven years old. We were just sitting and talking when we were approached by Blay-fry.

Blay-fry was departing his home, which was across the street and up on a slight incline from my house. While descending from his home, he noticed the children and me in the yard, and as he got closer, he said, "Looks like you got yourself three monkeys there." I was shocked by what this idiot had said. I looked at the children and gathered my thoughts. I turned to French-fry and said, "Actually, I've got three hunters, and we were waiting on an idiot, and our guest just arrived."

I immediately turned to the children and tried to explain to them what had just happened. I remember telling them what that statement meant and explaining to them the monkey comparison that racist people have placed on the African-descended people.

Monkey Comparison

This is an excerpt from the Science Blog on February 8, 2008, showing that the depiction of African-descended people as apelike had disappeared from mainstream US culture. Research presented by psychologists from Stanford, Pennsylvania State University, and the University of California-Berkeley reveals that many Americans (white people) subconsciously associate blacks with apes. In addition, the finding showed that society is more likely to condone violence against African-descended criminal suspects as a result of a broader inability to accept African descendants as fully human, according to the researchers.

Jennifer Eberhardt, a Stanford associate professor of psychology, who is black, was one of the researchers. She was shocked by the result, particularly since they involved subjects born after Jim Crow and the civil rights movement. "This was actually some of the most depressing work I have done," she said. "This shook me up. You have suspicions when you work—intuitions. You have a hunch. But it was hard to prepare for how strong the black-ape association was, and how are we able to pick up every time?"

This is how: "So God created man in his own image, in the image of God he created him, male and female he created them" (Genesis 1:27).

When you hear someone make such a statement or reserve that belief, you can believe he or she is not of good spirits but of evil spirits. A person with this thought pattern also calls God a lie in this prejudiced view.

Chapter 3

CAREER

Military and Criminal Justice

I started a life of employment upon my graduation from high school. I joined the Texas National Guard. I stayed a Texas Guard member for approximately two and a half years and then transferred to active duty. I joined the US Army active duty in 1987. My military job was a logistics solider, and I was responsible for unit readiness by maintaining the unit's weapons, equipment, and accountability records. My first duty station while on active duty was in South Korea.

I was later assigned to the Eighth Field Artillery (10/92 FA), a unit within the Second Infantry Brigade. This was the most educating unit that I was a member of, because we all got along—black, white, Asian, all nationalities. It was my first time spending any personal time with someone of another race, with exception of my basic training (BT) and advanced individual training (AIT). The difference between the training phase of the military and active duty is control. In the training phase, all movement, activity, and thoughts are controlled by the drill instructor. When you are on active duty, your life changes from controlled to free movement if you have a pass or are not on duty. The reason for the identification of the training phase versus the active-duty phase is to show the difference—how you are controlled in your environment in one, and in the other, you have the freedom to visit, engage, talk, and walk with whomever you want. In this unit, that's exactly what it was. We all hung out like brothers. There was so much brotherhood among everyone in the unit. We stayed in the field training most of the time, but we didn't mind; we had fun training.

In the Second Infantry Division, we worked five and a half days a week, Monday through Saturday at noon, and then we were off until Monday morning. We did a lot together as a unit. We would go on nature walks in the mountains in the local Korean communities. It was interesting to see their culture up close; it was very different from America. You would see the natives drying out red peppers and fish on the concrete. You could also see the rice patties and the farmer riding on what appeared to be rototiller with a wagon attached for his seat and his harvest. We walked through the streams that flowed down the hills. We partied together, all races of the armed forces. The United States has all branches of the armed forces in South Korea, so we all mingled. I made friends with blacks, whites, Koreans, Hispanics, everyone who was friendly. I even talked with the people who had the loner-type attitude. I would engage them too. One thing I found to be familiar was a stigma I thought I had left in Texas and the United States: racism.

Can you believe these racist people are taking their racist views, theories, and practices overseas? Yes, they are! I was shocked to find out that they have been spreading the myth about the African-descended man growing a tail at night to the wonderful people of South Korea. I was asked that question by a Korean woman. She said, "Do you grow tail?" She was a local shop owner on the street market, where venders gathered to sell souvenirs, blankets, shirts, shoes, and almost anything that could be handcrafted.

I was somewhat shocked by the question, but being from China, it was not as breathtaking as some of my previous experiences. I gathered myself, sort of laughed a little, and said, "Why did you ask me that?" She said, "The white GI tell me." I really laughed then and simply told the lady, "That's not true," asked her to visit Genesis 1:27, and moved on.

Genesis 1:27 says, "So God created man in his own image, in the image of God created he him; male and female created he them."

While stationed in Korea, I had the strangest thing happen to me. I was roommates with two white guys, and we were also coworkers; we all worked in the department of logistics. One of the guys was from New Jersey, and the other guy was from Portland, Maine. We had a triangle of personalities. I was optimistic, the Maine guy was daring and adventurous, and the guy from New Jersey was overbearing and aggressive.

In 1988 after spending a year in South Korea, I was transferred to Ft. Drum in Washington. I was thinking it was another artillery unit, but this one was a little different. It was an air defense unit. Air defense is an antiaircraft weapon, and Air

Defense also has female soldiers in the unit. Field artillery is used to support the army in the field or support infantry soldiers in active combat.

I spoke of the difference in the restrictions and the freedom of basic and active duty as I characterized how well everyone got along in Korea when I was assigned to the Second Infantry Brigade. I hate to draw this conclusion, but if I don't, you won't get the full picture of the inference that I am drawing. I can conclude that because of the foreign land we were on, we were limited in our ability to isolate into our own racial groups, because our freedom was limited. We had curfew and restrictive passes to leave post, and no one could just run and hang with their cultural comforts.

After spending a year in a foreign country and enjoying all that new brotherhood, I had forgotten about the separation in America. Ft. Drum welcomed me back home to America pretty quickly because I could see the separation. The soldiers tended to hang out with people of their own race, especially after duty hours.

I wouldn't call that racism or segregation. I would rather call that a part of American culture. America really has a problem trying to figure out how to infuse the African-descended people into its culture. That's interesting considering the melting pot that America has become! However, as you examine its diverse communities, you will never see an abundance of whites and blacks coexisting in residential areas—with the exception of some of the less fortunate whites who may or may not be employed and who just don't have the proper education to move into the more prestigious areas, or are maybe on drugs. What's more interesting than that is since 1909, the National Association for the Advancement of Colored People (NAACP) has long struggled to eliminate racial discrimination and segregation from American culture.

America and the world need to adhere to these words or die as fools: "And he made from one man every nation of mankind to live on all the face of the earth, having determined allotted periods and the boundaries of their dwelling place" Acts 17:26.

The next experience I'd like to share with you was one that gave me an opportunity to teach and become an ambassador for the African-descended people. I want you to take the challenge when you encounter a similar situation as in this next story. *Safety is the key. If it's not safe, don't try it.*

While stationed at Ft. Drum, I had the honor of meeting a young man by the name of Rex. Rex was a young white kid from Mississippi. He was about eighteen years old, stood about six feet tall, and weighed about 130 pounds wet. Rex was a very shy young man and wouldn't say very much unless you engaged him with a question or a statement. We were assigned to headquarter company and headquarter platoon, and your jobs in the military determine where you stay within a unit. Since Rex and I were in the same platoon, we stayed in the same barracks. So I had a lot of opportunities to engage with this young man, and it was very revealing. After spending some time with him, one thing I noticed about Rex was his shyness; he appeared to be more geared toward fear of the unknown. Why would I say that? Through my observation, I noticed Rex was more verbal and comfortable being around Caucasians and shy and reserved around me. At the time, I was the only African-descended person in the section. Trust me; when you are the minority in this world, you observe everything about everybody. I do it without any apology.

I explored his contrasting engagement between me and the Caucasians in the section and discovered several interesting things about Rex. The first shocking and very sad thing I learned about Rex was that he was a member of the KKK. That information saddened me to the core, especially after he told me the story of his family, his father in particular. I honestly can't remember how he came to tell me that he was a Klansman. The only way I can explain him opening up to me is I tried to be a good ambassador for the African-descended people, and in doing that, I guess he trusted me. I recall Rex telling me that he wasn't allowed to watch any African-descended television shows, particularly *The Cosby Show*, featuring Bill Cosby and a full cast of emerging young African-descended stars. The one thing I noticed while he told me that story was the look on his face; it was a look of regret and a sense that he had been denied an opportunity to explore his own prejudices. It appeared that if given an opportunity, he would have watched the show and enjoyed it.

Rex opened up to me and really fueled my drive to prove to him that people are the same regardless of race—good, bad, ugly, beautiful, arrogant, selfish, and so on. I remember teasing Rex about going home with him for Christmas, and we would laugh and say, "Yeah right," and we would say, "That wouldn't work out." It was obvious to me that Rex was raised to hate African-descended people by his father and maybe the whole family. When you hear of the research work from Jennifer Eberhardt, a Stanford associate professor, and how the ape/monkey comparison is still in the mind of many young Caucasians even today, it's because it's being taught by the parents, and it will always exist.

The challenge for the people that would like to see racism disappear is to become an ambassador for God and their race and promote good will among all they meet. You never know whom you might encounter. You may be able to change a Klan and make a friend. If you need more encouragement, read the following:

"Be imitators of me, as I am Christ" (1 Corinthians 11:1).

"Therefore, we are ambassadors for Christ, God making his appeal through us. We implore you on behalf of Christ, be reconciled to God" (2 Corinthians 5:20).

Kids Do Come with a Manual—The Technical Manual

Rex's father trained him to hate. Hopefully he'll find out someday that he was designed to love. The Bible has instructions for how to raise a good Christian child. The old story that kids don't come with a manual is false. The

Bible is the instructional manual for human beings. This instructional manual teaches you how to live as a God-fearing, loving person. It tells you how to operate. It properly teaches you how to act and raise your children. Here are a couple of instructions for parents:

"Train up a child the way he should go; even when he is old, he will not depart from it" (Proverbs 22:6).

"Folly is bound up in the heart of a child, but the rod of discipline drives it far from him" (Proverbs 22:15). Folly is defined as the lack of good sense or judgment, or foolish behavior.

"Fathers, do not provoke your children to anger, but bring them up in the discipline and instruction of the Lord" (Ephesians 6:4).

Today ends that old saying that kids don't come with an instructional manual; they do, and so do you. It's called the Bible.

End of Service?

I was scheduled to end my tour of duty in the military in 1991, but in 1990 the Gulf War / Desert Storm happened. That had more consequences than just the potential for going to war; for some, it meant not being released from an active-duty tour/contract when it ended. The army put a freeze on anyone getting out of the Army. If you were scheduled to get out, as I was, you could legally be held past the time of your contractual obligation.

This really didn't sit well with me because I didn't feel like I had any control over my life at the time. I was due to get out the military as planned after four years of honorable duty and return to my civilian status. Once the army instituted the freeze and stopped allowing anyone to get out, all that changed, and so did my passion to remain in the military. I did what any honorable solider did or would have done; I reenlisted for another four years.

Along with my reenlistment, I also had an opportunity to get reclassified in a new skill, so I chose to become an heavy-equipment operator. I reenlisted and got orders to attend a six-month course at the Combat Engineer Corps in Ft. Dix, New Jersey, where I was trained as a heavy-equipment operator. I was trained to operate a bulldozer, grader, scraper, bucket loader, and dump truck. I graduated top of the class and as an honor graduate.

I returned to Ft. Drum after graduating from the US Army Engineering School and was reassigned to a remote base in Alaska. This was a very unique unit in many ways. It was a sub installation to a larger installation, and we had a split command—administrative and tactical, and split installation. We integrated with the civilian governmental employees and maintained two installations, one consisting of a live-fire small-arms weapon range. They were, in essence, part of our unit.

Dog Days

The unit and installation played a major role in the support of army reserves, national guards, and local law-enforcement agencies. We offered training areas for field-training exercises for military components and also buildings for urban tactical training for law enforcement and military tactical units.

We also offered various small-arms live-fire qualification ranges. They ranged from twenty-five yards to three hundred yards. The ranges were all automated, which means they automatically recorded the hits on the target by the shooter without human manipulation, and it recorded the score for the shooter without human manipulation, thus providing the most accurate and sterile qualification.

I was assigned to range control, which had command and control of the daily operation of the ranges and the sub installation. The installation consisted of civilian and military personnel. The military rank structure was as follows at range control: one staff sergeant, one sergeant, one specialist (P), and another specialist.

First-distinction specialist (P) means you have met all the criteria to be promoted to the next grade of sergeant, and the specialist without the P for promotable is still considered an enlisted, whereas the promotable is considered a junior noncommissioned officer. There is an old saying in the Army (RHIP), rank has its privileges, but there is a clause, and that would be if the P is attached to an African-descended person, then you have some leeway on the RHIP when it defies the white privilege. That was the basis of my first assignment. There was a challenge to get the white specialist in a sergeant position. It was between a young, white golden boy and me. I guess I was the adopted little brother.

The dilemma was due to a sergeant departure and my assignment to replace the sergeant because I was promotable. I was to be placed in his departed position, which was the scheduling (NCO) noncommissioned officer and sergeant position. They wanted the white specialist to have the position.

The Test

I didn't realize it at the time, but the NCO who was in charge of the military personnel had given me a test—okay, not really, just a stupid excuse not to allow me to work as the scheduling NCO. He had given me some type of personnel form to fill out to get stuff like next of kin, whom to contact in case of an emergency, and so on. It also requested information about my home address, and this is where I messed up my opportunity to work as the scheduling NCO. I either misspelled a word or didn't capitalize it. At any rate, that was the reason he gave me for putting the young white specialist in that position. I didn't want to tell this genius that the system was equipped with a spell checker.

The other position that was available at the time was a range inspector position, and I just knew I was going to get that position since they had given my assignment to the less qualified white specialist. I was fed some feel-good feces to get me to look at another position that was supposed to be reserved for the civilian wage-grade worker. An example of the work they did was keeping the installation grass cut on the ranges and around the barracks and other facilities. They used the fact that I had gone to the heavy-equipment operator school to lure me into taking that position under false pretense and lies.

Lies You Tell

They told me if I took the position with the civilian worker, I would have an opportunity to get my journeymen licenses/certification as a heavy-equipment operator, and they would help me enroll in the program. They also ensured me that I would get the hours on the equipment needed for the journeyman's title. Each thing I mention that they said to me was a lie, and the only piece of equipment I ever used was the tractor with a bush hog or a lawn cutter attached to it. Once I accepted the position, all I received was scrutiny. This was by design; they had to come up with reasons to keep me from doing what they had offered to do, which was give me an opportunity to succeed and get my training.

I found out that I was being monitored and watched each morning. I would be answering questions like, did you lock the gate after duty? Did you put gas in the van, tractor?

Cutting grass ended up being my full-time duty. I'm talking over a couple of hundreds of acres of grass and open field. I would cut the grass from morning to close of business, as we say in the Army (COB), which was usually after everyone else had gone home. This particular evening, I had scratched one of the equipment-building doors. This happened around five or six a.m. in the evening, and no one was at the installation except me. No one was there to report it to, and as a matter of fact, I didn't think much of it since there was no structure damage and just a scratch on the door approximately six inches long.

The following morning when I arrived at work at approximately six, I had a surprise and a court date with the kangaroos. Well, not really kangaroos but what is known as a kangaroo court. It is a judicial tribunal or assembly that blatantly disregards standards of law or justice and often carries little to no official standing.

When I entered the building, I was greeted by this mob. There was a counter, and it was enclosed with a gate entrance. On the other side of the counter were five white men sitting in various positions and places—one sitting on top of the desk, a couple leaning back in their chairs, and a couple with their feet on top of the desk with the look of authority, power, and pure spite. I also want to point out one of the civilian workers was an sergeant major in the reserve, and the sergeant major is the highest enlisted rank in the Army. He was also in charge of the civilian workers and me, as I was assigned to cut the grass on the installation. Prior to my arrival, the civilian workers cut the grass.

The reason I pointed out the military status and rank of this civilian employee as an sergeant major is that he should have used what is commonly called tact to make the correction, if that was the intent of this court. This is one of the major roles of an sergeant major. The sergeant major is all about troop morale, accountability, fairness, and supporting the solider. He also serves as a liaison between the enlisted soldiers and those who are noncommissioned and the commissioned officers appointed over them.

Earlier in the book, I spoke of another kangaroo court I experienced in high school with the football coaches, and I referred it as my first kangaroo experience. I recognized the setting immediately when I saw these white men assembled to accuse, charge, and deliver punishment. When you encounter this type of playing field with such influential people involved (an head football coach and an sergeant major of the Army), it's very intimidating and just squeezes all the hope you have of getting a fair chance. I had no chance of redemption.

To understand how great or not so great my chances were, consider the following hypothetical situation, which demonstrates what it feels like to have no faith: Two young African-descended men were walking home one day late in the evening. A young white man, a civilian employee, Was driving down the road. He was intoxicated, and he ran over the two of them and killed them. One of the victims ended up in the cab of the truck, and the other victim ended up a hundred yards down the street. The sheriff arrived on the scene and found the young white man crying and saying, "I am going to spend the rest of my life in prison." The sheriff slapped the young white man and said, "Listen. This is how we're going to do this. The suspect that's inside the cab, we will get him for breaking and entering, and the suspect down the street, we will get him for leaving the scene of a crime. Now go home, young man, and get some rest." That's what my chances felt like in both of those situations. I had no chance.

I think the sergeant in charge of the military personnel asked me if I knew what happened to the equipment room door. Taken back by the question, I just sort of stood there for a second before saying yes. They started to imply that I tried to hide the incident. I really didn't understand what was happening until I was informed that I wouldn't be allowed to operate any of the other equipment. That meant I wouldn't be able to train and get my hours needed for my journeyman certificate. Was that the motive behind this? Maybe not! However, it was certainly the result of their decision and action.

Betrayal

Thank God for his blessing. With God's help, I didn't fret. In fact, I expected this type of betrayal. You might say betrayal is a strong trait to place on a person's character. You can't be betrayed by a stranger; only someone close to you can betray you. What can you do when you are betrayed?

Matthew 6:14–15 says, "For if you forgive others their trespasses, your heavenly Father will also forgive you, but if you do not forgive others their trespasses, neither will your Father forgive your trespasses."

John 13:21 says, "After saying these things, Jesus was troubled in his spirit and testified, 'Truly, truly, I say to you, one of you will betray me.'"

Luke 22:48 says, "But Jesus said to him, 'Judas, would you betray the Son of Man with a kiss?'"

Man, isn't that chilling? The Son of Man asking you, "Would you betray me?" That's a question we all need to ask ourselves today. Finally, this last verse isn't an old saying; it is the word of God. "So whatever you wish that others would do to you, do also to them, for this is the Law and the Prophets" (Matthew 7:12).

So, yes, do unto others as you would have them do to you!

I thank God for the peace of mind to keep me positive during this tremendous time. One might ask why I didn't file a complaint or report these incidents. Well, there were a number of reason, and they were not limited to fear. The most important reason for dealing with this type of ignorance was that I wasn't just living for myself at the time. I was starting a family, and my actions had to line up with the needs of my family. The most important need for my family was for this father to be able to support his family, because these idiots were always going to be idiots. I tell people, "Sometimes you've got to think for other people," especially idiots."

God has always been with me, even in times I wasn't aware of his presence. He was there with me guiding me with these words: "Therefore he who is prudent will keep silent in such a time, for it is an evil time" (Amos 5:13). Prudent is defined as carefully providing for the future, and I can assure you that I wasn't alone in that room that day. God had my back and kept me silent.

One thing about the military that most soldiers really enjoy is the opportunity to travel and meet new people. It wasn't very long before one of the court members received orders to transfer to another unit, and one of the sergeants was scheduled to get out of the army. This placed a strain on the unit and the schedule, with a shortage of range inspectors.

Remember the test with the misspelled word or wrong capitalization? It wasn't an issue anymore; he decided to place the specialist in the range inspector position and me as the scheduling NCO. Funny how that happened. I should also tell you that as time went on, I also became a range inspector. I didn't understand what the problem was. I excelled in every duty and every task that was assigned to me. They didn't do anything to me except keep me in prayer, and when you pray and have faith, it's like being with God!

Promotion

I was promoted to sergeant in 1992. First, getting promoted in the Army to sergeant is equal to a civilian employee going from the assistant manager to the manger. The Army has a tradition of doing promotional ceremonies. I want you to brace yourself for this one. The sergeant in charge of the range inspectors came to me and asked, "Do you want a promotional ceremony?" I said, "Of course I do!" He made it seem like it was going to be a problem to have what is a normal activity in the Army, a promotional ceremony. That's all I'll say on that.

Transfer Orders

I received orders to transfer to another unit outside of the United States, and I didn't want to leave my family, and the plan to get certified as a journeyman heavy-equipment operator had been terminated. It was time to make a major decision to exit the military, and I needed a plan and fast.

While working as an range inspector, I had an opportunity to meet an older African-descended man who was in the army reserves and also worked as a correction officer for the adjacent state. He was an easygoing man and a pleasure to talk to. He told me about his career as a correction officer and how much he enjoyed it. I was very interested in correction after speaking with this nice gentleman.

I explored a couple avenues to get the training necessary to become an effective correction officer. While still pulling my shift as a range inspector for the army, I attended one of the local schools, going to classes four nights a week. I received a diploma as a certified correction officer and graduated with honors.

As soon as I graduated from the school, I started applying for positions in that field but received no response. I then contacted that nice gentleman I had met at the base while he was training. I told him I had attended the school and was certified as a correction officer. He gave me a couple of numbers, and like my friend Ben says, "Look what God did for me, man."

We got the job! I was hired for the job in March 1995, and it took me until May 12, 1995 to process out of the Army. On May 13, 1995, I was on duty at 6:00 a.m. as a correction officer, the very next day after getting out of the Army. I didn't spend even one day unemployed, thank God. God inspired the security manager at the time to allow me to process out the Army for approximately two months. He saved the job for me; God guided him. You can do want you want and plan what you want, but you must remember: "We can make our plans, but the Lord determine our steps" (Proverbs 16:9). And no one can stop what God has planned for you if you keep your faith in him and don't give up. My goal was to provide for my family, and God didn't allow me to fall into the grips of the devil's work.

Their plan failed, and they placed me in a blessing.

The Blessing of Serving

While working in the correctional system, you see a lot of grief and pain, and people feeling like they have no rights. You also hear them complain about the officers in charge of them, harassing them and restricting their opportunities.

How? They restrict opportunities by issuing conduct reports for things as simple as an inmate protesting disrespect from an officer. Example might look like this: Officer orders an inmate to clean the restroom, but he doesn't address the inmate by his name; he uses a moniker (a nickname), and the inmate responds, "Sir, please don't call me that. You know my name." The officer responds with, "Are you being argumentative?" Inmate responds, "No, sir, I just want to be called by my name." Officer responds, "You got an eight-hour bunk in," which means the inmate is restricted to his bunk or room for eight hours, except to use the restroom if it's not in the room and to go to the institution dining room for meals.

That simple interaction can create many other restrictions, and if the officer can illustrate in his report that this inmate poses a danger, it can restrict him to institutional settings only. The reason I said institutional settings is because some inmates can earn enough good reports that they are able to participate in work-release programs, jobs that are outside of the institution gates, such as road crews and park crews. They also assist with fire support for the local fire agencies during fire season and many other various jobs.

The reason I called this a blessing is because it reminded me of the path that I had traveled to that point—experiencing a lot of grief and pain, and people having no regards for my rights. It's one thing to experience these things yourself, but to see and to hear it happening to someone else touched my heart in a way that I can't explain.

I am a veteran, and it embarrasses me to see what so many people go through after so many of us veterans risked so much, some even dying to protect our rights! If you don't respect the people, respect the veteran who risked his life for all racist and peaceful people.

I can say one thing; it inspired me to be a better person. I have never told an inmate that I love him, but every time I saw them cry about their despair, my heart would just feel as if it was crying with them. I really had a genuine concern for their health, safety, and general welfare.

When I say I cared for their well-being, I mean every inmate that I ever supervised or encountered, regardless of race or beliefs. I made it my business to let them know that I cared, and it wasn't just verbal. I demonstrated it while I performed my duties around them, with them, and for them.

I wanted to be a good and fair leader for the inmates and myself, and to explain it better, I will direct you to the following passages:

Message to Law Enforcement

Exodus 18:21 says, "Moreover, look for able man from all the people, men who fear God, who are trustworthy and hate bribe, and place such men over the people as chief of thousands, of hundreds, of fifties, and of tens."

I believe if we are to change the problem we have in law enforcement in the world today, it is imperative that we seek out men who fear God. If you think you are superior, this job isn't for you. As a public servant, you must have humility.

Philippians 2:3 says, "Do nothing from rivalry or conceit, but in humility count other more significant than yourselves."

The blessing I spoke of earlier was the gift of service. I realized why I was placed in the position as a correction officer. I believe God wanted me to realize my gift.

I really work every day with a heart of service.

While in the army, I recall reading a poster that stated, "You are not an interruption of my work; you are the purpose of my work." I took that to heart, and if you are in public service, adopt that slogan and put your responsibility above yourself.

For me, service means a lot of things, but I know who has the correct answer. Lets go to 1 Peter 4:10, "as each has received a gift, use it to serve one another, as good stewards of God's varied grace."

Galatians 5:13 says, "For you were called to freedom, brothers. Only do not use your freedom as an opportunity for the flesh, but through love serve one another."

Mark 10:45 says, "For even the Son of Man came not to be served but to serve, and to give his life as a ransom for many."

I'll drop the mike on that! Enough said. I love to serve and help others, and I do it with a joyful heart.

Proverbs 17:22 says, "A joyful heart is good medicine, but a crushed spirit dries up the bones."

And 1 Peter 4:9 says, "Show hospitality to one another without grumbling."

While working as the night supervisor at the institution, I had an inmate that wanted a friend to get a job on the night crew. The night crew basically cleaned the institution—sweeping, mopping, waxing, and buffing the floor at night, and other odd jobs after institutional lights were out.

The inmate that wanted me to hire his friend was a skinhead or a white supremacist. He had been working on the crew for approximately one month, and we really didn't talk much. I really tried to give inmates an opportunity to meet me through chance and not through a disciplinarian process. That being said, he didn't really know me either, so when he communicated to me about his friend getting a job, it wasn't verbal. He gave a note to an African-descended inmate to give to me. When I received the note, I asked the inmate that delivered it why the other inmate didn't bring it to me. He said he didn't think I wanted to talk to him. Of course I knew why! I asked the inmate to take the note back and have the white inmate bring it to me. It was a prime opportunity to get to know this young man.

The inmate departed, and some time passed, and the white inmate never came. We had our lunch breaks at midnight, and I decided if he didn't approach me before lunch, I would speak to him then. Ten minutes or so before we started our lunch break, he finally approached me and passed me the note. He intended to keep walking. I stopped him and asked him, "Why you didn't bring me the note in the beginning?" The inmate responded, "I didn't think you would talk to me." I asked why, and he kind of shrugged his shoulders and said, "You know." I then said, "Why? Because of your gang affiliation?" and he said, "Yes." He also had various racist tattoos on his body, including a double lightning bolt.

I took this opportunity to teach this young man about what I call the easy blessings of life. I started by asking him if I could get personal with him, and he said yes. I asked him, "What does your mother think about it?" The inmate stated that she didn't like it, and he said she worried about him. I told him that's what he should be concerned about—the way his mother felt about his involvement in a gang.

I went further to explain to him that if he didn't care about himself, he should at least be mindful of the stress his gang affiliation placed on his mother. For anyone who faces this situation, parent or child, be exposed to the truth: "A wise son makes a glad father, but a foolish son is a sorrow to his mother" (Proverbs 10:1).

Exodus 20:12 says, "Honor your father and your mother, that your days may be lone in the land that the lord your God is giving you."

Colossians 3:15 says, "Children, obey your parents in everything, for this pleases the Lord."

The reason I call it an easy blessing is because if the parent raises a child with love, discipline, and most importantly the word of God, he or she will not depart from it.

Proverbs 22:6 says, "Train up a child the way he should go; even when he is old, he will not depart from it."

The easiest thing anyone can do—would you agree?

One Blood

"Then the Lord God formed the man of dust from the ground and breathed into his nostrils the breathed of life, and the man became a living creature" (Genesis 2:7).

The following story is about another inmate that came to the institution with a history of being a white supremacist. He had a reputation that preceded him, and he had a long history of misconduct that included everything from gang activity, extortion, and assaults to gambling. I am a firm believer of giving someone an opportunity to show me who they are without having any preconceived notions of who they are based on others' opinions. When it comes to dealing with such a diverse and complicated prison community, you engage every inmate cautiously and respectful. I was able to navigate this tense and adversarial environment in a way that I was able to communicate with all the inmates, regardless of their misconduct history.

Shortly after arriving at the institution, this inmate was given a job as a janitor to clean the front of the institution. Remember the misconduct history of this inmate and his white-supremacist affiliation. His work assignment was just outside of the area that I worked in. That only fueled me to engage this inmate every time I saw him, as his job placed him in my path to the restroom. Every morning, I would speak to the young man, and he would return the morning greeting. I eventually stood outside and had small talks with him, and we would talk about anything, like the birds flying around the institution or just the simple life of a day.

One day this inmate was scheduled to be transported to the county court for a hearing. Prior to departing the institution, inmates have to be strip-searched, and they are strip-searched upon their return. On this particular day, I conducted the strip-search. Before I started the search, I asked the inmate if I could ask him a question. The inmate said yes, so I said, "If you were dying, and you needed a blood transfusion, and we had the same type of blood, would you let me help you"? He laughed and said "no". I laughed also and said, "Let us continue with the search." After we concluded the search, I said, "You really wouldn't let me help you?" and he just laughed and continued to the waiting room for transport.

Interesting that this young man would have rejected the opportunity to live if it meant receiving the blood of an African-descended person. Let us take a look at that ideology: "He made from one man (blood) every nation of men to dwell on all the face of the earth, and has determined their pre appointed times and the boundaries of their dwelling" (Acts 17:26). And "There is neither Jew nor Greek, there is neither slave nor free, there is no male or female, for we are all one in Christ Jesus" (Galatians 3:28).

I know there is a myth or strong belief in America that if you have three-fifths or one drop of blood from an African-descended person, you are classified as African. I hope that wasn't this young man's thinking, but if so, I pray that he changes and knows that we are one. To further illustrate how idiotic that belief or myth is—if the one drop or three-fifths rule was true, we might have to change our position of President Obama being the first African-descended president.

Your Participation Requested

I conducted my research on the statements listed below. However, I am leaving my opinions to myself. I understand my opinions to be just opinions, and they are in no way factual as they relate to these statements. I ask you to do your own research and come to your own conclusions if you are as curious as I am.

Let's start with the first president of the United States of America under the Continental Congress from 1781–1782 John Hanson was the president is he from African Descent and became President when the new country was actually formed in March 1, 1781 with the adoption of the Articles of Confederation. John Hanson is also credited with designing the presidential seal used today. What was his genealogy?

George Washington became President of the United States in 1789 after gaining impendence from Britain under the current US Constitution.

What about the third president? What was his genealogy?

What about the seventh president? What was his genealogy?

I have to give this next gentleman a bit of an introduction. His name comes with the nature of his existence at the time. He was able to free many, thus placing him as the father of a multitude of free people. He stood tall and was the sixteenth President in the White House. What was his genealogy?

I was intrigued by the information I gathered doing my research. It's amazing how the more you know sometimes only makes things more confusing. But that's only if you try to figure it out with your own understanding.

Proverbs 3:5 says, "Trust in the Lord with all your heart, and do not lean on your own understanding."

If you are still concerned or confused, as I am, remember to go back to Galatians 3:28: "There is neither Jew nor Greek, there is neither slave nor free, there is no male or female, for we are all one in Christ Jesus."

This is the conclusion of my correctional career, but it is in no way the last story I have. I have a book in mind about an incident that drove me out of law enforcement and eventually into retirement. It is a story filled with deception, lies, cover-ups, and conspiracy. Stay tuned.

Chapter 4

PARENTING

This portion of the book will focus on a couple of incidents that involved me as a parent. It will deal with law enforcement and will cover some interactions with educators.

Profiling

I have my opinion about the term profiling and what it means, especially as used by law enforcement. I'll keep the following in mind before I profile anyone: "Judge not, that you be not judged. For with what judgment you judge you will be judged, and with the measure you use it will be measured back to you" (Matthew 7:1–2).

The first incident I would like to tell is about the day my son was profiled by two gang-enforcement officers. The incident started out under suspicious circumstances and ended up concluding in my front yard. Yes, I looked out my window and saw police lights flashing behind the car parked in front of my house near my driveway. I identified the car that had been pulled over by the police as my son's car, and I went outside to see what was happening.

When I got outside, I could see my son, and I yelled to him to ask what happened as I walked down my driveway. He yelled back and said that the officer said he didn't put on a signal to turn into the drive.

I thought that was strange since we lived on a street that had little to no traffic. I was thinking safety couldn't have been the concern of the officer since the traffic action on the street was slow, and it is also a residential area.

I approached one of the officers. He was of Asian descent. I was communicating with him peacefully and casually. The other officer was a young white male. He was standing rigidly on the other side of the car, with his hand on his service belt. He seemed to be very tense or uncomfortable as he stood there with his dark sunglasses on. I want to know who decided that it was right for police officers to approach citizens with their sunglasses on. Take off your glasses! I want to see the eyes of the people who have sworn to protect me.

I then addressed my son and asked if he was all right, and he said yes. There were two other kids in the car, as they were returning from the park. I asked the police if they could get out of the car and come in the house, but they didn't allow them to leave.

My son then told me the police had followed them for about seven miles before citing him with a traffic violation. That was suspicious. Why was he following my son and his friends in his car for approximately seven miles? I asked the white police officer why he was following my son home. I also asked him what his probable cause was to follow my son in the first place. He gave me an answer that didn't pass the smell test; it smelled bad as soon as he open his mouth. He said, " As he passed us at the intersection, we noticed that he took his eyes off the road for a second." Yes, let it sink in for a minute. Tell him anything—ha! Not today.

I said, "You're telling me you saw my son pass you while you were at an intersection, and you saw him take his eyes off the road for a second, and that's enough for you to follow him home and charge him with a traffic violation? Come on, man. You're kidding me. I take my eyes off the road for seconds at a time, and I've never been followed for that." I have spoken to police officers. Guess what? They take their eyes off the road also. This guy wasn't being honest with me, so I asked him a direct question. "Are you profiling my son?" He said no. I then explained to him that if you believe something is going on, you should be honest with a parent. He assured me again that he wasn't profiling my son. I told him that I didn't believe him, and I requested that he call for his sergeant that was on shift.

The Asian police officer called for his sergeant, and some time passed before the sergeant arrived. While waiting, I had a chance to speak with the Asian officer alone; he seemed to want to tell me something. He appeared to be a very honest man, and I trust my evaluation of people. He really seemed genuine in his mannerisms. While I was communicating to the Asian officer, I turned and noticed the white officer staring at me intensely, now with both hands on his utility belt and giving me a mean mug. I informed him that he wasn't intimidating me by staring at me, and I advised him to stop staring at me.

I have made mistakes, and I consider that one of them. I want you to always respect officers and not do as I did.

Moments later, the sergeant arrived. I called my son to the rear of his vehicle where the officer's car was parked.

When the police sergeant exited the car, he went directly over and gave my son a handshake. Then he gave me a handshake. Let me show you how God works. He stepped back and said, "What's the problem, gentlemen?" I explained to the sergeant that I had asked his officers if they were profiling my son, and they said no, and I explained why I thought they were not telling me the truth.

This is when the police sergeant dropped the bomb on the officers. His first statement was "Yes, we are the gang unit, and they are two of my gang officers." His next statement was to his officers. He stated, "This isn't the kind of young man we're looking for," referring to my son. (The police sergeant had actually coached my son before as a football coach, even in an all-star football game). I believe he was sent there by God.

Psalm 91:11 says, "For he will command his angels concerning you to guard you in all your ways."

Psalm 34:7 says, "The angel of the Lord encamps around those who fear him, and delivers them."

The police sergeant and my son talked for a moment as I spoke to the two responding officers. One thing I tried to relay to the officers was that when you're dealing with someone's children, you should always be honest with the parents. I would further say it is your duty and responsibility. The problem with being honest in a fabricated incident is then the hold incident becomes a lie. This is how a traffic stop turns from just a traffic stop to a potential civil rights suit or worse—a use-of-force situation.

There was no probable cause to be followed in the first place. This is still a free country, and you don't need permission to move freely.

But remember, where there is trouble, God is near if you believe and carry your faith in everything you do.

Psalm 37:39 says, "His salvation of the righteous is from the Lord, he is their stronghold in the time of trouble."

Nahum 1:7 says, "The Lord is good, a stronghold in the day of trouble; he knows who take refuge in him."

Educators

Show yourself in all respect to be a model of good works, and in your teaching show integrity, dignity, and sound speech that cannot be condemned, so that an opponent may be put

to shame, having nothing evil to say about us.
(Titus 2:7–8)

This story will take you into the world of college sports and the obstacles one might face if he is of African descent.

Starting with the recruiting process, I knew this was going to be a challenge for my son and me. The school that he eventually went to was very interested in his talent in the classroom and on the gridiron. That being said, they gave him the most interest, and I wanted him to attend this school because of their academic reputation. The end of his senior year, he was selected for an in-state bowl game, and he had a stellar game. His participation in that game brought in more interest from other schools. My son took interest in one in particular, and we pondered what was best for him both academically and athletically. I was still in favor of the initial school, but my son was intrigued by the other school's division level. Now we were deciding between the two schools, so I told my son, "If you are considering this other school, you should let the coach of the initial school know." I thought that was the most courteous thing he could do since recruiting has a time period, and if you spend time on a recruit, and he changes his mind, it can really hurt a team's future success if the recruit is considered a top recruit.

I had my son make the call to the head coach. Early in the recruitment, I let the coach know I wanted my son at his school for the academic reputation. I even went as far as to tell him at some point that I wanted him to treat my son like he would his. Every time I spoke with this coach, I spoke of academics, and at no time did I engage in trash talk.

Now my son made the call and informed the coach of his dilemma. During the course of the conversation, the coach tried to convince my son his school was the best by using an analogy. He told my son, "I feel like the girlfriend that's done everything right, and this other school comes along like a beautiful stripper and gets your attention." My son told me what the coach said, and I said, "Are you kidding me? He knew you are an intelligent young man. He should have used a better analogy than that." In fact, I thought it was either disrespectful or a way to undermine my son's intelligence. Either way, it didn't sit right with me. I told my son I was going to call the coach and ask him why he didn't use a better analogy. I made the call, and he confirmed what he had said to my son and said he had no apology for it. He did say, "That's the way I feel." Let us look at the communication through God's eyes. I can't touch it since I miss communicated also.

Ephesians 4:29 says, "Let no corrupting talk come out of your mouth, but only such as is good for the building up, as fits the occasion, that it may give grace to those who hear."

Proverbs 16:24 says, "Gracious words are like a honeycomb, sweetness to the soul and health to the body."

Proverbs 15:1 says, "A soft answer turns away wrath, but a harsh word stirs up anger."

I communicated with the coach, and I'm sure I missed a lot of these points, just as he did in communication with my son.

Still holding strong to my son going to the initial school, I gave the coach an idea that could possibly seal the deal. I asked him to talk to the basketball coach and ask him to call my son. My son was also an outstanding high school basketball player. Needleless to say, after the basketball coach called, the deal was sealed. He played both sports and graduated on time.

He enrolled and was accepted in the initial school, and we ran into other issues with this particular coach. There's one I would like to share with you. I identify it as holding a man down—or a dream deferred.

The football season started, and everything was going great, especially after one game where my son touched the ball eight times and had approximately 208 yards. That game was leading up to the next week's game, which was the school's archrival. The winner would get a bid in the playoffs.

The game started, and the stadium was packed. Local television stations were on hand for the big game. During the first half of the game, my son did not touch the ball. I'm not even sure if he played in the first half. Our team was losing, and my son wasn't playing. I had parents come up to me and ask, "What's wrong with your son?" and I would say, "Nothing." They then asked what was going on.

I could tell my son was getting impatient by the expression on his face. When you are dealing with this type of person, its checkers; every move counts. I got his attention and gave him our signal for how to fix his expression; it was just a frown. The first half ended, and I had a chance to speak to him. I had to lift his rooted faith. I told him not to let this guy see his frustration, wich is what most humble and God-fearing people should do.

"Then he said to me, 'Fear not Daniel'" (Daniel 10:12).

I told him to go in the locker room and be excited and at no point show his frustration. I assume he did so, as the second half started with him getting the ball at least seven times, averaging at least ten yards each carry. At the conclusion of the game, he had seventy-seven yards. He had outrushed everyone who carried the ball in the first half, mostly white kids, some carrying the ball at least sixteen times. Because of this selfish move by the coach, we lost the game.

After the game, my son was steaming hot. I had to console him again. The coach had looked in his direction, and that gave my son the perception that he knew how he was feeling since he never addressed him after the game.

The first thing I needed my son to understand was that the coach could play who he wanted to when he wanted to. He understood the concept; the head coach determines the players' roles on a team.

Once we got past that part of our conversation, I advised him to ask the coach about the game in a couple of days. I told him to approach the coach in a matter-of-fact conversation, reminding the coach of the previous week's statistics. Eight touches for approximately 208 yards. I wanted him to speak to the coach with a calm head and have a set of questions in mind so that he didn't offend the coach.

The most important thing I wanted him to understand was that this thing he was going through would be part of what he would have to endure. One must understand early in life that there will be trails and thing that will challenge your humanity. I wanted him to understand in order for him to become someone that could withstand a lot of pressure. I also wanted him to understand that it was very important not to let this guy see his emotions. I wanted him to demonstrate respect in his approach and to be firm.

On Wednesday following the game, he had the opportunity to speak to the coach. The coach's response to my son's question was the most ridiculous thing you could imagine coming from a professional coach. His response to why he didn't give my son the ball until the second half was, "I don't want you to think you are a prima donna." Now I thought this guy was really disrespecting my son; look up prima donna and see how it's defined.

Every coach that ever coached my son was always impressed with his respectful attitude and would agree that he was nothing of a prima donna—just competitive, never boisterous.

I simply told my son that if he didn't feel comfortable with the answer and didn't feel that he was being respected, I would attend a meeting with him. I also told him he could say anything he wanted to as long as he was being respectful.

I think it took about three weeks, and the meeting was arranged. Prior to the meeting, I told my son to say anything he wanted to because I wanted him to handle this matter. After all, he would have to live with the result.

What I admired more than anything was his willingness to risk his opportunity to play a sport over what he felt was an unfair practice or a preconceived perception from another person. With that in mind, he had my full support. Remember, he went to college for an education. I wanted him to understand the full scope of the American educational system, down to its basic perception of our young African-descended men. The coach had already labeled my son as a selfish person by referring to his potential actions as those of a prima donna—which is someone who's vain or conceited!

The day of the meeting, we went to the head coach's office. As we entered his office, there was a waiting room where it appeared all of the assistant coaches had assembled. I thought that was weird since this meeting took place is the midst of the recruiting season.

We proceeded to the office, and the meeting began. My son started the meeting by mentioning the comment from the coach, referring to him as a prima donna. The coach excused himself to my son, saying, "I'm not used to players questioning me about football. I'm usually talking to them about family issues."

I had told my son that I wasn't going to say anything, but I had to respond to his comment and his excuse. I let the coach understand that my son has parents, and he didn't necessarily need his parental guidance from him—just his fairness. I asked him, "Do you want me to talk to him about football?" He didn't respond to the question, so I said, "We're here to talk to you about football, and you're the coach, and I'm the parent."

Another incident happened while my son was in school that proved you couldn't trust or depend on this coach. My son was in a vehicular accident while in college. I had to be at work the day of his court appearance, but I wanted someone to be there as his support.

I called this head coach and asked if he could attend the traffic court with my son or have someone present with him. I got off the phone with this guy, thinking he didn't give me a good feeling of support for my son. With that in mind, I asked for the day off from work and was able to attend the traffic hearing. Good thing I did; the coach was nowhere to be seen. Every time the court door opened, I would turn and look with the hope that he wouldn't let his player down like this, not to mention the parents. He did let his player down. He was a no-show, and what was worse than that was he never mentioned it, and neither did I. So when you use a blanket lie to answer a young man's question, yes, the parent is supposed to speak up, and I did. He wasn't family friendly, at least not to my son. I concluded my statement, and I returned to my position as a listening and supportive parent.

My son brought up another incident to the coach where he felt the coach treated him differently from other players, particular white players who played the same position as my son. I tried to get him to understand the possible reasoning of the coaches, and it was positive. I told my son, "The reason the coach pointed you out is because he probably thought if he could say it to you, then everyone else could accept some criticism." I was trying to encourage him to be a leader and to also learn to accept criticism. I probably should have asked what was he feeling instead of encouraging him to be strong. What do you think? I realize now he was experiencing institutional racism—just as I did!

My son was referring to a game where the weather was adverse. It was raining. Rain during a football game creates a lot of problems, including fumbling. My son asked the coach about that game. "Why did you yell at me when I only fumbled the ball once and recovered it, and two of the white guys fumbled the ball and didn't recover it, and you didn't say anything to them?" The coach's response to that was, "I didn't think you were so sensitive." Again, I had to intervene.

I interrupted the conversation. I said, "Hey, excuse me, you need to learn how to listen. You have a young man here trying to express himself to you, and you're sitting here making conjectures. You need to listen and not make conjectures." His response to me was, "Mr. Accuracy, are you upset with me?"

I said, "No, I'm not upset with you, but I should be with the way you are disrespecting my son. If it was up to me, he would never play for you again."

Then I turned to my son and said, "You can do what you want in this situation. I won't make that decision for you." Then I turned to the coach and said, "I will let my son make his decision about playing for you in the future." The meeting finished, and we departed the office.

The following season, my son didn't play football, and the following season, the coach transferred a different school as the head football coach.

What message can be taken from this story? I don't have all the answers. Part of the reason for this book is for me to lay down these stories and see what messages God has laid forth for me. Let me start with a couple that have helped me understand this incident. The coach wanted to know if I was angry with him. I wasn't. I already knew who he was, and I wouldn't give him that satisfaction. I wanted him to listen and think. I had learned from James 1:19: "Know this, my beloved brother; let every person be quick to hear (listen), slow to speak, and slow to anger."

These elements were all at play during that meeting, and because of my mother teaching me not to be angry, I can only take you here: "Train up a child in the way he should go; even when he is old, he will not depart from it" (Proverbs 22:6).

My teaching to my son was and will always be *know the nature of the beast*. He wanted me to be angry, and he wanted my son to be an out-of-control African-descended male. No way.

Conclusion

I hope and pray that what you have read in this book did not offend you. If this book offended you, I would ask that you take an inventory of yourself because you may be leaning toward the wrong side of humanity.

This book is being presented in good faith, with the love of all of mankind. It is not my role to determine who is good or evil, but I can express my experiences, and I can be factual and actual in my presentation of these stories. I tell these stories not to separate; I write them to help teach our youth how to respond to racism in a positive way.

I would be remiss if I didn't end with the following experience.

The man I love more than any other was a white man. He was my friend, he was my dad, and he was my first sergeant—Top, as we called him.

Top, you are the one man who gave me an opportunity to trust the white man. I thank you for being an ambassador for your race and God. I thank you for everything you did for me. Most importantly, thanks for never making me feel like I was different. While I was writing this book, I was informed that you had passed away and gone home. I look forward to seeing you in heaven so I can thank you personally.

My only regret in preparing this book is that some will read this and be confused as to who the victim is. As I heard one man say of the president, "The president could watch a cowboy movie and couldn't tell you who the bad guys were." Everybody knows the cowboy is the bad guy; you can't take people's property and call them bad. They defend their families, humanity, and properties, and they are called the bad guys.

It's like calling African-descended people the bad guys because they defend their families, humanity, and properties. When you watch a movie about gangsters and police, who is the bad guy? Art imitates life.

"And the Lord was sorry that he had made man on earth, and it grieved him to his heart" (Genesis 6:6).

I believe he is grieving now.

Visit the Authors website, I like to hear from you.

http://www.trainedtohatebutdesignedtolove.com/

Printed in the United States
By Bookmasters